BATS
A NATURE-FACT BOOK

by
D.J. Arneson

Cover photo: Animals Animals/Earth Sciences

Interior photos: Merlin D. Tuttle,
Bat Conservation International, Inc.
P.O. Box 162603, Austin, TX 78716

Special thanks to Dr. Merlin Tuttle and Janet Debelak
of the Bat Conservation International for their help.

Copyright © 1992 Kidsbooks, Inc.
7004 N. California Ave.
Chicago, IL 60645

ISBN: 1-56156-147-9

All rights reserved including the right
of reproduction in whole or in part in any form.

Manufactured in the United States of America.

WHAT ARE BATS?

*When the sun goes down on a summer night,
the bats come out and cause a fright.*

Bats were made for the night, but they're not scary at all. They're shy, gentle animals that are greatly misunderstood. Not many people really get to know them. When they do, they discover that bats are among nature's most interesting and helpful creatures.

Bats are mammals, the only ones that can fly. Their bodies are covered with fur that may be black, brown, gray, red, or yellow. Bat wings are naked or lightly furred with sensitive hairs. Bats give birth to living young and take care of their babies until they are old enough to survive on their own. Bats have teeth to crush and cut food and feet with strong, hooked claws for grasping.

Bats are nocturnal. They sleep during the day, hanging upside down in trees, caves, or other safe places and are active at night. Most bats have extraordinary hearing. By hearing echoes of their own cries, microbats (insect-eating bats) can safely fly in pitch darkness to find the food they need to survive. Megabats (fruit-eating bats) rely on their sense of smell and sight.

There are almost a thousand kinds of bats in the world. Most live in warm or tropical regions. None live where it is extremely hot or cold all year long. Forty-three kinds of bats live in the United States. They live in forests, fields, deserts, and even in cities.

Large bats weigh as much as four pounds. The smallest, the bumblebee bat, weighs less than a penny!

As you'll see, bats—even vampires—are much more than flying shadows in the night.

Roosting, but wide-awake, Gambian epauleted megabats.

HOW DO BATS FLY?

Millions of years ago, bat ancestors were small, insect-eating animals that lived in trees. Maybe they were like today's tiny shrews. Slowly, a sheet of skin grew between their legs and body. When an early bat stretched its legs, the skin tightened to form simple wings. The wings were only good for gliding from limb to limb. After thousands of years, bats learned to flap their wings and could truly fly like birds.

A bat's wing is a thin, stretchable membrane made of two layers of skin. It is very strong, but thin enough to see through when held up to a strong light. Most bats' wings have no fur or hair, and certainly none have feathers. The membrane is attached to the bat's four extremely long "fingers," its forearms, its body, and its rear legs. When the bat extends its wings, the membrane stretches tight. When the wings are folded, the membrane relaxes into tight wrinkles, like an umbrella covered with rubbery fabric.

To fly, a bat spreads its arms and legs to form wings and then flaps its forearms. To control its flight, the bat flexes or bends its long fingers to change the curve or shape of its wing. Bats with a membrane between their rear legs use it as a rudder to help steer.

Bats are not as strong fliers as birds, but they are much quicker and more agile. They twist and turn with amazing speed without losing control. Some bats fly slowly. Others can rip through the air at 45 miles per hour and even faster with a tailwind.

Bats wrap themselves in their wings to keep warm, or spread them wide to cool off. They also use their wings to catch insects, as you will see.

A lesser long-nosed bat in flight.

HOW DO BATS SEE IN THE DARK?

Most bats feed after the sun goes down. This isn't a problem for fruit-eaters who use their sense of smell to find food. But insect-eaters must locate and catch tiny flying insects to survive. You may wonder how bats see their prey after the sun goes down. It isn't seeing at all. It's a specialized kind of hearing called *echolocation* (eko-lo-ca-shun) or bat sonar.

Microbats make high-pitched squeaks as they fly. The sound is made in the bat's throat and comes out of its nose or mouth. That's why most pictures show bats with their mouths open. They are squeaking. The sound is too high for humans to hear. Sound is caused by vibrations of air. You can feel vibrations when you touch your nose and hum.

People can hear sounds up to 20,000 vibrations per second. A bat can hear 200,000 vibrations per second! Scientists think each bat makes and hears its own sounds. That may explain how one bat can find its way in a bat-filled cave.

A bat searching for insects sends out 20-30 squeaks per second. The sound travels in front of the bat. If it strikes something, it bounces back to the bat's sensitive ears. The ears may be small and round, long and pointed, or thin or wide. Some are fur-covered and others are naked. The ears are set far apart and each one can hear different sounds. The bat hears the echo and flies toward the object. It increases its squeaks to 200 per second. The closer the bat gets to its prey, the faster the sound returns to its ears.

Using echolocation, a bat can find a mosquito flying six feet away and close in for the catch!

A bat catches an unsuspecting moth in mid-air.

WHERE DO BATS LIVE?

Scientists think the first bats lived in tropical regions, and most still do. Others live all over the world, except in extreme desert or polar regions. Some even live within a few miles of the Arctic Circle. There are about 200 kinds of megabats. They live only in the tropics of Asia, Africa, and Australia. There are 800 kinds of microbats and most live in the tropics. The bats of North America are microbats.

Most kinds of bats live where it is warm and food is plentiful all year. Cold weather makes life difficult for bats because insects and fruit don't survive big temperature changes. When winter approaches, bats either fly to where it's warm (migrate) or find a safe, comfortable place to sleep until spring (hibernate).

In warm weather, bats roost (rest or sleep) in trees or protected places like caves, barns, and attics. They hang upside down by their hind legs. They sleep during the day and come out at dusk to hunt. Some return to the same roost before dawn, while others find a new roost each night. Several, like red bats, roost alone in trees. Others roost in caves in colonies of thousands and even millions. Bracken Cave in Texas has a colony of twenty *million* Mexican free-tailed bats! It takes almost four hours for the whole colony to leave the cave even though over 80 thousand fly out every minute! Philippine bamboo bats sleep in hollow bamboo plant stems. Some South American bats hide under palm leaves they bend into tents.

Caves are favorite roosting and hibernating places. They are dark and secluded and have just the right temperature and humidity bats need.

Roosting gray-headed flying foxes.

WHAT DO BATS EAT?

Each kind of bat has its own diet, from bugs and bananas, to frogs, fish, and flower nectar. Most microbats, the kind that live in the United States, eat insects. Most megabats, the kind that live in tropical regions, eat fruit.

If you have bats where you live, you'll see them searching for gnats, flies, beetles, moths, or mosquitoes at dusk. They swoop and dive, listening for echoes bounced off their unknowing prey. They home in on the bug. As the bat gets close, it throws its legs forward and spreads them. The wings and the membrane between its rear legs form a shallow pouch. When the insect is close enough, the bat catches it with its mouth and eats it or flips it into the pouch with its wing tip. It then dips its head into the pouch and snaps up the insect. In one night a bat may eat half its own weight in insects. Together, the Bracken Cave bats can eat 250 *tons* of food in a single night!

Fruit bats eat mangoes, bananas, peaches, and other tropical fruits. Most fruit bats find their food by smell and sight and do not need echolocation.

The bulldog bat of Mexico, Central, and South America uses echolocation to detect ripples on water. The ripples signal that a fish is under the surface. The bat grabs the fish with its claws, chews it into pieces, and stores them in cheek pouches as it hunts for more.

The lesser long-nosed bat and other flower bats lap nectar from flowers with their tongues and eat the pollen that sticks to their fur.

False vampire bats eat blood and meat. Their prey includes frogs, lizards, birds, and even small animals. And, of course, true vampire bats feed only on blood!

A bulldog bat uses echolocation to find its prey.

WHERE DO BATS GO IN WINTER?

Bats that live in warm climates can find food all year long. They have no need to travel. Many spend their whole lives in one area. Bats that live in regions that have winter cannot survive because their food supply vanishes with the cold. They must migrate (fly to somewhere warm) or hibernate until spring.

Migrating bats fly south on the same flyways (flight paths) used by migrating birds. They usually fly at night. Some, like the red bats that spend summers in Canada and winters in Mexico, fly thousands of miles.

Most North American bats hibernate in winter caves where they live on stored body fat. Since bats are small to begin with, the fat supply is also small.

Winter caves cannot be too hot or too cold, too wet or too dry. The temperature is usually 35 to 50 degrees Fahrenheit. If the temperature drops below freezing, most kinds of bats will die. Some kinds can survive temperatures in the low 20s. If the temperature rises, the bats wake up. If they become too active, they use up their stored fat and may die of starvation if there isn't enough left to last until spring. For this reason it is very important never to disturb hibernating bats.

An active bat breathes 200 times a minute. Its heart beats 13 times a second and its body temperature is high. A hibernating bat breathes 20 times a minute, its heart beats only 15-20 times a minute, and its temperature drops to 50 degrees Fahrenheit.

A cave may have thousands of hibernating bats hanging from its ceiling. Nobody knows how bats can tell when spring arrives, but when it does, they wake up and fly to their summer roosting grounds.

Mexican free-tailed bats fill the evening sky.

BABY BATS

Most kinds of bats have only one baby, although some have two. The parents mate in the fall, before hibernation. The baby is born in the spring after the mother wakes up from hibernation.

Some bats have their babies alone. Others have their babies in nursery colonies. Nursery colonies are in warm areas where food is plentiful. Bats usually return to the same colony every year.

In May or June, when a female bat is ready to give birth to her baby, she reverses her usual roosting position. Instead of hanging head down, she hooks her short thumbs onto the roost. She curls the membrane between her hind legs to form a safety net to catch the newborn baby. The mother cleans the baby and then returns to her normal, upside down position. The baby clings tightly to its mother's fur. If it falls, its mother cannot pick it up and the baby will die.

A newborn bat is typically born hairless, blind, and hungry. It has oversized feet and claws to help it cling and hang. It immediately crawls up its mother's body to nurse. The mother feeds it until it is big enough to hunt on its own. At first, the baby remains at its mother's breast even when the mother flies out for food. Each mother nurses only her own young.

In a few days the baby's eyes open and it can see. In about two weeks it is too heavy to carry. The mother hangs it on the roost to wait for her return. When the baby is about three weeks old, it is strong enough to fly and hunt by itself.

A healthy bat may live for 16 years or more. Some have lived over 32 years!

A Mexican free-tailed bat and her baby. Note the baby's huge feet and claws.

MICROBATS

Scientists separate bats into two groups. Small bats are called microbats (micro means small). Large bats are called megabats (mega means large).

Most kinds of bats are microbats. There are over 800 kinds and they live almost everywhere in the world except very hot and very cold regions.

All 43 kinds of North American bats are microbats. The most common are big brown bats and little brown bats. Little brown bats are seen at dusk flying around houses. One of the rarest is the spotted bat. It lives in deserts of the American southwest. Mexican free-tailed bats also live in the southwestern United States.

Except for some meat-eating bats such as the false vampire bats, with a wingspan of over 32 inches, most microbats are small. The world's smallest mammal, the bumblebee bat of Thailand, is a microbat. It weighs less than a penny and can sit in a teaspoon. Pipistrelle bats, common in many countries, are so small that one hundred of them weigh just one pound.

North American microbats weigh from a quarter to a whole ounce, although some weigh a half pound, the same as two sticks of butter. They are an inch and a half to three inches long from head to tail.

Most microbats are insect-eaters and use echolocation to hunt. They live in areas where their favorite insects thrive. Little brown bats like mosquitoes, so they often live near water. Big brown bats roost near fields and shaded lanes where the bugs they like live.

Microbats' favorite roosting places are caves and abandoned mines. A single cave can hold millions.

Two elusive and seldom seen spotted bats.

MEGABATS

Megabats are also called fruit bats because they feed on fruit, flowers, nectar, and pollen. They are the largest bats in the world. Some have bodies that are two feet long with six-foot wingspans. Some weigh four pounds! The smallest megabat, the southern blossom bat, weighs just a half ounce!

The largest megabats are the flying foxes, called that because their faces resemble foxes. They have large eyes, pointed ears, and are covered with reddish, brown, tan, or gray fur. Almost 200 kinds of flying foxes have been discovered so far.

Megabats live only in hot regions of Africa, Australia, and Southeast Asia. They live in groups, called camps, hanging in trees and orchards by the thousands. Some fruit bat camps are fifty years old.

Megabats rest during the day and feed at night. They fan themselves to keep cool and often squabble noisily. Fruit bats leave their roosts just before sunset and return just before the sun comes up.

Megabats don't need to chase their food as microbats do, so they don't need echolocation. Only one megabat, the Rousette bat, uses a primitive type of echolocation. All others rely on their senses of sight and smell to locate food. Also, since megabats live in hot climates where there is plenty of food all year long, they don't have to migrate or hibernate.

Fruit bats have good vision and can see well even in the dark. They use their strong sense of smell to locate food. They eat avocados, bananas, peaches, mangoes, and other tropical fruits. Some drink nectar from flowers like overgrown hummingbirds.

A megabat eating a ripe fig.

VAMPIRE BATS

Vampire bats are the most feared bats in the world. There are three kinds of true vampires. They feed on sleeping, warm-blooded animals, and sometimes even people. That's what makes them so scary.

Vampires live only in Mexico, and Central and South America. They roost in caves, cracks in rocks, and hollow trees, and hunt at night. Unlike other bats, they can crawl, hop, leap, and scamper over the ground on all fours as quick as a crab. This lets them creep up on their victims, or, if discovered, jump to safety.

The best-known vampire bat is the small, reddish-brown or gray-brown common vampire bat. It's about three inches long and weighs about an ounce. It feeds on the blood of cattle. It has excellent eyesight and can spot a cow in a pasture at night over 400 feet away!

The other two vampires are not very well known. The hairy-legged vampire prefers bird's blood. The white-winged vampire feeds on bird and goat blood.

The common vampire bat's face is pushed in so its snout doesn't get in the way when it's feeding. It has two long, triangular incisor teeth in its upper jaw. Its lower lip is split so its tongue can lick freely when feeding.

Vampire bats hunt by sight, but can use echolocation to avoid obstacles. They land near or on their prey and are usually unnoticed. They cut a small, circular wound in the animal and wait for the blood to pool. Their saliva has a chemical that prevents blood from clotting. They lap the blood until they are full, usually about an ounce. Several bats may feed from a single bite.

Victims that die after vampire bites die of rabies, not the bite.

A rare close-up view of a vampire bat. Note its sharp teeth and split lip.

BATS AND THE ENVIRONMENT

Every creature in nature has a place, and bats are no different. They are among the most helpful animals. They are also some of the most misunderstood because people overlook the good and remember the bad.

There are about a thousand different kinds of bats living all over the world. Almost seventy-five percent, the microbats, eat insects. About thirty percent, the megabats, feed on fruit and flowers. Only vampire bats drink blood. False vampires eat meat.

A single microbat the size of a field mouse weighs only about an ounce. It can eat as many as 600 mosquitos an hour. In one night, it eats about one-third its own weight in insects. A nursing little brown bat can eat *more* than its own weigh each night.

A thousand bats eat about 20 pounds of insects a night. In a single season from May through August, that can add up to over a ton! One colony of free-tailed bats living in Texas eats more than 6,000 tons of insects a year. Insects might not rule the world if there were no bats, but they surely would rule the night.

At least 300 different tropical forest plants rely on bats to survive. Like bees, megabats that eat nectar fly from flower to flower in search of food. Pollen from the flowers sticks to their fur and is carried to the next flower. The pollen rubs off on the new flower, and the plant is *pollinated*. If a plant is not pollinated, it cannot produce seeds.

Some wild fruit trees depend on bats to spread their seeds. Fruit-eaters chew the fruit for its juice but spit out the seeds. The seed sprouts to make a new tree.

That flying bat you see is not harmful, it's helpful.

A lesser long-nosed bat approaches a cactus flower for its nectar.

BATS' ENEMIES

Hawks, falcons, owls, snakes, and raccoons are among bats' enemies, but people are their worst. People kill more bats than all their natural enemies.

Bats rely on night and fast flight for protection. They can usually outfly an airborne enemy. Bats are in most danger just before the sun goes down. Owls wait by bat cave entrances at dusk for their dinner. When the bats fly out, the owls strike. If one bat isn't enough, the owls return for more. A single owl once caught and ate 27 bats in one night!

Poisons and insecticides are serious threats to bats. In some places, bats are considered pests and are killed to protect fruit trees or cattle. Fruit-eaters eat ripe and over-ripe fruit. They are not a threat to growers who pick green fruit. Vampire bats are a threat to cattle and must be controlled, but thousands of innocent bats may be killed to control a harmful few.

Insecticides used to control insects also kill bats. When bats eat insects containing insecticides, the poison gets into the bats' bodies. If enough poison is eaten, the bats die. Insecticide in bat mothers' milk is passed to nursing baby bats and the babies die.

In some places, people eat bats. A three or four pound fruit bat makes a meal. They are easy to find and catch because they are noisy and roost in trees.

Hibernating bats are often killed by thoughtless people. Disturbed bats may not have enough energy to survive until spring. Three boys once killed thousands of rare bats by knocking them down with sticks.

Bats should be left alone, for everyone's safety, including the bats'.

A group of bats roosting on a cave wall.

BATS AND PEOPLE

Bats are peaceful creatures and are more helpful than harmful. In some places, they are important to local economies and regional environments.

During the Second World War, scientists wanted to attach tiny firebombs to bats and release them over enemy cities. The bats would roost in buildings. When the firebombs went off, the buildings would burn down. The idea worked, but the plan was scrapped.

Bat droppings (guano) are an excellent source of nitrogen and make a high-quality fertilizer. Guano has been mined for many years. Some deposits on bat cave floors are hundreds of years old and many feet deep. Chemicals from guano were used to make gunpowder during the American Civil War.

People shouldn't keep bats as pets because few know how to care for them. Also, a bat that can be caught may be sick and should be left alone. Bats are even difficult to keep in zoos. Insect-eaters often stop eating in captivity.

Bats and other wild animals are associated with rabies, a serious disease. It is spread when an infected animal bites another animal. Unlike other mammals, a bat with rabies is rarely aggressive. Therefore, it's not a good idea to handle any bat.

Scientists study bats' echolocation to learn how this super sonar might lead to ways to help the blind. Bats' hearing is studied to help understand human hearing. Chemicals in vampire bat saliva are studied to find a blood-thinner. Blood thinners are used in the fight against heart disease and strokes.

Everyone can benefit from bats.

A fruit bat with a mouthful of fresh fruit.

INTERESTING BAT FACTS

The earliest known bat lived over 50 million years ago. Bats have changed very little since then. About a thousand species (distinct kinds) are known. Scientists think many bat species remain undiscovered.

Bats come in many colors. They can be black, gray, red, yellow, chestnut, orange, and even white. Albino (pure white) bats are extremely rare. Some bats have many colors. Bats that live in caves tend to be dull-colored. Bats that roost in trees are often brightly colored with striking markings. The brownish hoary bat has black-rimmed ears, dark wings with orange markings, and white-tipped fur that looks like frost. The painted bat has fluffy, brilliant orange fur and solid black wings with orange markings. When it is roosting, it looks like a red leaf.

Some bats live alone. Most live in colonies that may include tens of millions of bats. Some colonies have lived in the same caves for thousands of years.

Most bats have short tails or no tails at all. Mouse-tailed bats have tails almost as long as their bodies.

Bats are excellent fliers. Most bats are not very good gliders, but megabats glide well. Bats also use their wings like blankets to keep warm and flap them while roosting to cool off.

Insect-eaters have sharp, pointed teeth for catching bugs and flat teeth for crushing and chewing. Vampires use their sharp front teeth for cutting skin. Fruit-eaters have chisel-like teeth for cutting fruit and flat teeth for crushing the pulp.

Hibernating bats breathe so slowly, they can live an hour without oxygen.

While this fruit bat sips nectar, pollen sticks to its fur.

NORTH AMERICAN BATS

If you live in the United States or Canada, you may see these bats, if you're lucky! All are insect-eaters.

Little brown bat—Familiar across the U.S. and Canada and lives near ponds and streams. It is about three and a half inches long and weighs about a fourth of an ounce. You might find one or more in an attic, a hollow tree, or in the cracks of rocks.

Big brown bat—Ranges over most of the U.S. and Mexico. They live near where they were born and don't migrate. They hibernate in caves, mines, cliffsides, hollow trees, and attics. The last bats you see in the fall and the first ones you see in the spring are probably big brown bats.

Gray bat—Named for their gray fur. They live and hibernate in large caves in Alabama, Missouri, Tennessee, and Kentucky. A single bat can catch and eat three thousand bugs a night! They are rare and endangered.

Red bat—The most common bat in many places, red bats live in most of the U.S. except the Pacific Northwest. They are rusty-red in color and roost in trees where they look like dead leaves. They can fly forty miles an hour and migrate long distances.

Mexican free-tailed bat—Live in huge colonies in large caves in the Southwestern U.S. With a tailwind, they can fly sixty miles an hour at high altitudes and travel as many as fifty miles to feed. A mother feeds the first baby that reaches it when she returns from feeding. This is called herd feeding. Free-tailed bats sometimes fly a thousand miles when they migrate south for winter.

Indiana bat—Found mostly in just four caves from Vermont to the Ozark Mountains. They are rare because millions died when people disturbed their hibernation.

The red bat is found in most parts of the United States.

The bumble bee bat is the world's smallest mammal.